Common Problems with the Elderly Confused

INCONTINENCE & INAPPROPRIATE URINATING

Graham Stokes

BA, MSc, PhD, ABPsS

Series Editor: Una P Holden

WINSLOW PRESS

Telford Road, Bicester, Oxon OX6 0TS   Telephone (0869) 244644

First published in 1987 by
Winslow Press, Telford Road, Bicester, Oxon OX6 0TS
Reprinted 1987, 1988, 1989, 1990, 1991, 1993

© Graham Stokes, 1987

ISBN 0 86388 056 8

WP152/Printed in Great Britain by Hobbs the Printers, Southampton

CONTENTS

Dr Graham Stokes is a senior clinical psychologist at Walsgrave Hospital, Coventry, with special responsibility for psychology services to the elderly. He graduated from the University of Leeds in 1976 and obtained his doctorate and qualification in clinical psychology at the University of Birmingham. Since qualifying he has worked in the field of adult mental health and now specialises in the psychological management of the confused elderly.

SECTION 1

Discovery

Can Nothing be Done?

As elderly confused people slowly lose touch with reality and become increasingly dependent, so caring for them can seem to be a never ending task of watching and worrying. Often problems mount up so that supporters have little time to relax and reflect upon what is happening. Unfortunately, the situation can deteriorate rapidly should the confused person become incontinent and start to urinate in the 'wrong' places. This is one of the most difficult and disturbing problems carers have to face and such behaviour can become 'the last straw'. Tolerance can wither like the fruit on the vine and feelings of disillusionment and resentment often appear.

Why is it that incontinence and inappropriate urinating is a common and major problem in the care of the dementing aged? Why is it that incontinence occurs relatively early in some people while for others it represents the end-point of a slow intellectual decline? There is no simple answer to this question. Greater understanding of this distressing problem—upsetting for both the elderly confused as well as their carers—has revealed a multiple pathway to toileting difficulties. As with other disruptive problems among the confused elderly, toileting problems can be a result of deteriorating memory and declining intellectual ability which not only affects the ability of elderly confused people to remain continent, but makes it increasingly likely that they will be unable to recall that they have urinated inappropriately. However, consideration must also be given to factors other than changes in memory for there may be alternative health, mobility, emotional or environmental reasons which may be responsible for, or be contributing toward the toileting difficulties.

Family Care

Incontinence and inappropriate urinating can be very distressing for relatives managing at home. It is not just the fact that the old person may not be able to control micturition (the technical term for the act of passing urine) that upsets supporters, but it is the problems that can result when confused old people are unaware of what they are doing which causes so much of the distress. The mess and unpleasant smell which is caused when a loved one urinates, for example, in the corners of the bedroom with little apparent regard for the feelings of the carer, can lead to a breakdown in goodwill. The act may even be perceived as a deliberate attempt to inconvenience or cause upset. Then there is the workload of washing and bathing the sufferer, the handling of soiled clothes and bedlinen, as well as the expense of laundering.

Even worse can be the attempts that are made to conceal the evidence of the act when some awareness remains. Instead of rinsing soiled underwear the person may wrap it in newspaper and hide it in a drawer. When subsequently found by the carer it is probable that the confused person will indignantly deny having put it there, and may even be angered by such an accusation.

For these reasons incontinence is one of the most demanding problems for supporters. Feelings of hopelessness, embarrassment, frustration and anger are commonly felt. Humiliated by their loved one's incontinence, carers often retreat from entertaining visitors. The resulting loneliness only adds to the misery. However, to their credit the majority of carers soldier on through each day, simply taking each problem as it comes and seeing what they can do. Yet for a minority the excessive strain of coping can lead to a break in the bond between dependent and caregiver, and sometimes to a request for residential or hospital care.

Institutional Care

Many of the residents of ordinary residential homes who are suffering from a dementia will also be incontinent of urine. Thus, the strain of caring not only affects relatives struggling to cope with the problem at home, but can also lead to feelings of frustration and despair among care staff.

In hospital, around 50 per cent of patients in psychogeriatric wards have been found to be regularly incontinent of urine, with a further 20 per cent occasionally incontinent. Often this is a major reason for admission of elderly people to long-stay hospital beds. While it is easy to regret the inability and unwillingness of some families to cope with incontinent relatives, these people may also be shunned or stigmatized by professional carers.

Many residential homes, while managing incontinence which occurs after admission, have a policy of refusing admission to old people already known to be incontinent. Although this is regrettable, such reluctance is understandable given present staffing levels and the existing degree of training care attendants receive in the management of incontinent residents. Staff concerned with improving the quality of life for the elderly people in their care have their objectives rendered impossible if they have to direct constant attention to keeping confused residents clean, dry and regularly toileted. Amongst nurses on psychogeriatric wards there is likely to be a sense of demoralization and irritation at the heavy drain on nursing time incontinence management involves. The 'toileting-round' can easily become a never-ending routine inexorably progressing through the day, leaving little time for anything other than a concern for the physical requirements of the patients.

The need for specialist skills to cope with the problem of incontinence and inappropriate urinating is clear. The more a carer understands about the reasons for the behaviour the better equipped he or she will be to manage the situation effectively. Unfortunately, many people believe that there is little that can be done when incontinence occurs in a memory-damaged person. However, such a point of view indicates a lack of interest in, and awareness of, modern methods of assessment, treatment and management. Incontinence need not be something which carers and sufferers must 'learn to live with', for appropriate intervention will often bring about some improvement and may lead to regaining of control.

It is the purpose of this book to give practical help to nurses, care staff and relatives on managing this complex disability. While its primary concern is with the problem of urinary incontinence much of what is described is also applicable to the even more distressing and poorly tolerated, and fortunately less common, handicap of faecal incontinence. However, it should be borne in mind that as this problem is more likely to occur in the severely confused it is less easy to obtain a therapeutic response and thus the hope that appropriate bowel movements can be restored must be tempered with caution.

Keyword Summary

Incontinence and inappropriate urinating
- A common and difficult problem
- Why does it occur?
- Multiple pathways

Family care
- Distressing behaviours associated with incontinence
- Feelings of hopelessness, embarrassment and frustration
- Excessive strain of coping

Institutional care
- Despair among care staff
- Incontinence is a major reason for admission
- Shunned by professional carers
- A time-consuming problem

Specialist skills
- Understanding the problem
- Improvement is possible
- Practical help for nurses, care staff and relatives

Faecal incontinence

Why is it Happening?

It is wrong to assume that all old people are alike simply because they are elderly. Similarly, it is a mistake to think that all those who are incontinent have toileting difficulties for exactly the same reasons thus raising identical management problems. Incontinence may have a single cause, or may be due to a subtle combination of factors each requiring a different response from staff or relatives.

Normal micturition involves the ability to store and void urine at will in suitable places and at convenient times. Elderly people may experience a need to void urine with greater frequency. Disturbance of this process will result in incontinence. However, it is advantageous to discriminate between incontinence as a condition whereby the person is unaware of their action, and inappropriate urinating which is characterised by a failure to void appropriately following recognition of the need to urinate.

Definition of Incontinence

Urinary incontinence denotes a failure of the mechanisms associated with normal storage and voiding of urine so that *involuntary* passing of urine occurs in inappropriate places or at inappropriate times.

Possible Explanations

Localised physical abnormality

Incontinence may result from local disorders of the urinary tract, and in such instances will require medical examination (in all cases of incontinence this is an advisable starting point). The manner of clinical presentation can result in a diagnosis of stress incontinence (involuntary loss of urine that occurs on physical exertion), urge incontinence (involuntary loss of urine associated with an uncontrollable strong desire to void which has not been anticipated) or overflow incontinence (the retention of urine with involuntary overflow). Consideration should also be given to the problem of constipation which is a common cause of urinary incontinence in the elderly.

Secondary nocturnal enuresis

It is possible for a person to experience bed-wetting after many years of complete control. This may be caused by sleep weakening bladder control or the problem may become apparent after the prescription of night-time sedation which impairs awareness of the need to micturate and so causes bed-wetting.

Loss of bladder control

Incontinence can arise directly from the loss of learned bladder control as a result of cortical atrophy affecting the frontal lobe. The outcome can be continuous incontinence. This may be inevitable in the advanced stages of dementia.

Definition of Inappropriate Urinating

Characterised by an *awareness* of a need to urinate which does not result in the voiding of urine at a suitable time in a suitable receptacle.

Disorientation

Incontinence can apparently occur following arrival at a new placement. A person who is unfamiliar with their surroundings may roam around the building searching for the toilet until they are compelled to urinate inappropriately. Even when a person has lived for many years in the same house they can become disoriented as their memory loss worsens.

Environment-induced

Even when the confused person is aware of the location of the toilet the design and layout of a building may make reaching the toilet difficult. The outcome of the 'race' between bladder and legs may depend on the distance which has to be covered and the confidence the aged person possesses to avoid obstacles which may clutter the way. If the elderly person should suffer from poor eyesight the task can appear insurmountable.

Loss of goal activity

A confused person may get up with the objective of using the toilet, but then forget what they had intended to do, leaving them walking aimlessly with no obvious motive until they urinate wherever they may be standing. The more confused and forgetful an elderly person is the less they will be affected by their incontinence.

Mobility and dexterity

Incontinence may the indirect consequence of physical disability. Although able to recognise the need to use the toilet, the confused elderly person may be prevented from doing so because of unsteadiness while walking or standing, or because of slowness in moving. Alternatively, the aged person may reach the toilet in time but may be incontinent because of dressing problems or an inability to deal with doors, locks, seats, etc. For example, the effects of arthritis or tremor associated with Parkinson's Disease may seriously interfere with the ability to perform skillful movements of the hands.

Emotionality

The onset of toileting difficulties may be associated with the experience of emotional trauma such as bereavement, rejection or movement to a new placement. The psychological basis of the problem may be either anxiety or depressed indifference.

Apathy

Continence is an acquired habit, the motivation for which may diminish among the confused aged as a result of quite minor factors. For example, unpleasantly low temperature in the toilet area or uncomfortable facilities may make the difference between continence and incontinence.

Attention-seeking

Through being incontinent a person who is receiving less attention than usual or an amount insufficient for their needs can manipulate carers and force them to take more notice and give more of their time. Incontinence may even be used as a means of revenge on those they wish to provoke or annoy.

Over-dependency

Over-concern by a carer may lead to the needless 'babying' of a confused person. The outcome can be a regression to dependent infantile behaviour characterised by incontinence.

Drug effects

Toileting difficulties may be a sign of drug side-effects. For example, persistent incontinence may be attributable to the excessive drowsiness caused by the use of tranquillizers, or may be an unwanted response of a patient to diuretics.

As you can see, incontinence and inappropriate urinating are by no means straightforward problems to either understand or manage. Nor can they be considered to be the preserve of the elderly confused.

Keyword Summary

Incontinence and inappropriate urinating
- Many causes
- Definitions
- Incontinence = involuntary behaviour
- Inappropriate urinating = awareness of need

Possible explanations:
Incontinence
- Localised physical abnormality
- Secondary nocturnal enuresis
- Loss of bladder control

Inappropriate urinating
- Disorientation
- Environment-induced
- Loss of goal activity
- Mobility and dexterity
- Emotionality
- Apathy
- Attention-seeking
- Over-dependency
- Drug effects

Not the preserve of the elderly confused

Making Matters Worse

Whilst intellectual deterioration, immobility and ill health all contribute to the problems of incontinence and inappropriate urinating, when seeking a more complete explanation we must clearly take into account environmental influences and appreciate the extra problems inadequate living arrangements and unwise management procedures can bring about.

Institutional Settings

In some homes for the elderly inappropriate urinating may arise as a result of unhelpful design features; the 'race' between bladder and legs is undoubtedly prejudiced by an excessive distance to the toilet and poorly designed chairs which make the journey difficult to initiate; similarly high beds may be a critical factor in the occurrence of bed-wetting.

The vast empty spaces on many hospital wards may seem never ending to a frail old person faced with the prospect of finding their way to the toilet. Highly polished non-slip vinyl flooring may appear to an elderly person with poor eyesight as wet and unsafe. Alternatively, a lounge which looks homely and inviting may in reality be an obstacle course of armchairs, occasional tables and rugs. The risks involved in negotiating these problems may outweigh the dislike of being wet or soiled.

Inadequate lighting en route to, and inside, the toilet area may discourage continence as will cold conditions and a lack of privacy. If there is no distinction between male and female toilets the prospect of embarrassing incidents can act as a further disincentive. Too few toilets (for the confused elderly are unlikely to be able to queue and wait), narrow toilets which do not accommodate walking aids and heavy toilet doors which constitute a formidable barrier to the frail elderly also contribute toward environment-induced incontinence.

As few institutions have adequate orientation cues the layout of a building can easily generate disoriented behaviour. Uniform colour schemes and a lack of directional information makes it difficult for memory-impaired residents to find their way from one location to another. Long, similar corridors with identical doors to bedrooms, bathrooms and toilets distinguished only by numbers or small name plates can result in residents 'wandering' because of bladder discomfort in search of toilet facilities that are difficult to locate. In a desperate attempt to seek a solution to an ever-pressing problem the risk of a resident urinating inappropriately in any available receptacle is high.

Depriving people of cherished possessions which offer both continuity with the past and reassurance can give rise to a feeling of distressing insecurity. Such an unpleasant break with personal history can easily make elderly confused residents feel anxious and depressed. The result can be an apparent deterioration in self-care abilities, when they have in reality simply lost the will, for example, to remain continent.

Physical Handicaps

A large number of old people suffer from poor mobility and impaired eyesight yet these handicaps are often left unattended, and are not considered relevant when considering why a person may be urinating inappropriately. The incontinent behaviour is often simply attributed to the fact that the resident is confused and is seen to be yet another sign of the process of deterioration.

Such a misguided assessment of the problem also means that a GP may not be asked to initially examine the resident in case the cause may be a comparatively minor and treatable medical disorder. Thus, a simple problem can continue to cause frustration and discomfort just because the appropriate remedial action was not taken.

The System of Care

Although living together with other people, an elderly resident has on average as little as eight minutes conversation each hour. This is usually with other residents—staff normally spend time with residents only when they are 'doing' something for them. Unfortunately, those residents who are the most confused tend to be even less involved and are therefore more likely to be ignored; that is, until they commit an unwanted act. Giving excessive attention to a person who is incontinent, even if it is borne out of a wish to appear caring, can lead to an increase in the inappropriate behaviour, especially if this is the only time individual attention is given.

A task-oriented rather than a client-oriented approach to care is likely to involve a rigid adherence to a programme of toileting. This increases the likelihood that staff will be available only during the toileting round and on those occasions when a resident has an accident and requires a change of clothing. If the care regime dictates that special areas in the home are set aside for incontinent residents, in order that the staff will find the task of incontinence management less arduous, the outcome can be even worse. As a large proportion of scarce staff time is being given to these incontinent 'sufferers', other residents may resort to incontinence to gain personal attention from carers. Alternatively, residents may make toilet requests which are unnecessary. If the staff response to such 'false alarms' is to toilet the person, then the unwarranted requests will be repeated, thereby increasing the drain on manpower resources.

Highly regimented toileting of all patients in order to prevent incontinence before an accident occurs not only encourages dependence, but by treating all residents as a homogenous group indicates that staff have not taken into account the individual needs of residents. A lack of consideration for the elderly confused is also illustrated when a resident is left on the toilet for ages, or when the toilet door is left open thereby exposing the resident to public curiosity. Such negative consequences of toilet use will only serve to discourage continence.

The use of incontinence pads during the day is undignified and can cause a loss of self-respect and embarrassment to the resident. Their use also creates apathy among both staff and resident as the consequences of being wet are less troublesome. The outcome can so easily be elderly residents sitting in a secluded area of a lounge being allowed to doze and wet.

Unpredictable toileting routines can often do more harm than good, as can the employment of different management ideas at the same time. In both cases the outcome can be misunderstanding between staff and heightened confusion among the elderly residents. Besides inconsistent work practices, another example of an unhelpful staff action is the inappropriate use of sedatives and tranquillizers which can easily turn a fit, if confused, old person into a drowsy and dependent patient.

As the problem of incontinence becomes increasingly difficult to manage, often there is a change of placement. Attendance at a day centre may be arranged or respite care in a hospital or residential setting may be requested to allow relatives a period of rest. Alternatively, an incontinent resident may be moved to another unit. While the reasons for these actions are understandable, as a failing memory makes it difficult for the elderly confused to adjust to strange and often unhelpful environments, frequent changes serve to increase disorientation, stress and thus the likelihood of inappropriate urinating.

Living at Home

Finally, while it is easy to see how problems can unintentionally arise in an institutional setting, when an old person lives at home their circumstances can promote inappropriate urinating to an even greater extent.

It is rare for furniture to be designed so that everyone, including confused elderly people with mobility problems, can use them. Chairs are likely to be deep seated and low, and the bed soft and difficult to climb out of. A severe and often insuperable environmental difficulty is when continence requires the use of a toilet situated at the top of a flight of stairs, or even worse, when it is situated outside. The toilet is also extremely unlikely to be designed for walking aids.

If the confused person has to spend hours at a time with little to do, possibly alone and feeling neglected or abandoned, this may serve to precipitate incontinent behaviour in an effort to gain revenge. If a relative, under strain from the burden of caring, is compelled to respond to their loved one's incontinence in order to maintain hygienic conditions, the inevitable increase in attention can result in the unintentional encouragement of the behaviour the carer wishes to avoid.

Possibly the most unhelpful living arrangement is when the confused person lives alone. Little contact with other people to provide stimulation and a tie with reality means that the confused person can become so disoriented that difficult management problems are to be expected. Living in a house which has been familiar for years as the family home is no guarantee that the elderly confused person will not eventually regard it as a strange and mysterious environment. As their memory progressively fails, agitation and anxiety can replace feelings of security and safety and result in stress-related incontinence.

In the beginning evidence of inappropriate urinating may be completely concealed. Soiled sheets may be hidden and newspapers or rugs may lie in various places on the carpet to hide damp patches. It is only when outside supporters discover the evidence or the smell of urine becomes prominent that remedial action can be attempted. However, with nobody to keep a watch on the confused person and provide information and assistance, unless the condition can be resolved through medical intervention, attempts to restore continent behaviour may be an uphill struggle.

You can probably think of many other ways in which incontinence and inappropriate urinating can be unwittingly encouraged and management made more arduous.

Keyword Summary

Institutional settings – environmental influences
- Unhelpful design features
- Unforeseen obstacles
- Inadequate toilet facilities
- Lack of orientation cues
- Loss of personal possessions and mementoes

Physical handicaps
- Poor mobility
- Impaired eyesight
- The need for a medical examination

The system of care
- Loneliness
- Giving excessive attention to incontinent behaviour
- Task-oriented v. client-oriented care
- Damaging toileting procedures
- Neglect of the *individual*
- The negative use of incontinence pads
- Inconsistent work practices
- The inappropriate use of medication
- Frequent changes of placement

Living at home
- Severe environmental difficulties
- Isolated and 'abandoned'
- Unintentional encouragement of incontinence
- Living alone:
  - few ties with reality
  - disoriented and insecure
  - the difficulty of resolving the problem

Understanding the Individual Problem

Before tackling the problem of incontinence and inappropriate urinating it is important to recognise that while you can describe the reason for the problem in general terms (eg. secondary nocturnal enuresis, environment-induced, apathy), it must ultimately be seen as an example of unwanted behaviour *unique* to an *individual*. We therefore need to have a thorough understanding of the elderly person's toileting difficulty as it is occurring *now*. Do not rely on guesswork or on an opinion based on a previous episode of incontinence.

What is Causing the Behaviour?

Appropriate toileting is a complex process requiring a number of skills. These are:

- recognising the need to micturate
- being motivated to use the toilet
- postponing, within limits, the onset of micturition
- locating the toilet (or acceptable alternative)
- possessing the physical mobility to get there on time and being able to adjust clothing appropriately
- maintaining goal-oriented behaviour
- initiating micturition when toilet is reached

The chain of behaviours can break down at any point because of personal deficits, institutional factors or a mixture of both.

In order to understand why the confused person is having toileting difficulties, we need to examine the situations in which these difficulties occur. Each episode of incontinence needs a thorough investigation to identify the particular behavioural difficulties involved. This involves identifying when and where the behaviour takes place, noting what the person was doing at the time they were incontinent and what the response of carers was to the incident. This task can be easily carried out by following the *ABC analysis of behaviour.*

A = Activating event or situation
B = Behaviour (in this case incontinence and inappropriate urinating)
C = Consequence

Examples of questions which need to be answered under these headings are:

A
- What precipitated the person's apparent incontinence?
- Does it occur at a specific time of day; after a meal; in a certain location; after a visitor has gone; when a particular member of staff is on duty; when the person has not been prompted to toilet; or when the elderly person is on the way to the toilet?
- Did it follow a request to be toileted?
- What was happening around them at the time?

B ● What form did the incident take?
● Is it a full bladder discharge, or dribbling?
● Where did it occur? In their clothing or in a receptacle (eg. fire bucket, wash basin)?
● Was the person unaware of their incontinence, or were they agitated, distressed or indifferent toward the incident?

C ● What was the response of carers to the incontinence?
● What was said to the person?
● What was the reaction of other residents?
● Did the incontinent resident attract the attention of carers to the incident?
● Did the person help to wash the wet clothing or dispose of any soiled linen?
● What was the person's response to the attention of carers?

The ABC's are recorded each time an incident of incontinence and inappropriate unrinating occurs. All carers should be aware that the behaviour is being observed. It is best to record the information at the time of the incident as it is easy to forget the exact circumstances if the recording is left until later.

As you can see, a Behavioural Analysis provides an accurate and detailed description of actual behaviour in terms of how often it occurred, the circumstances in which it arose and the consequences for the resident with toileting difficulties. However, the need for a comprehensive analysis means that two further areas of information need to be obtained.

Background

First, it is essential to record the background to the problem, including medical and nutritional variables, in order to effectively understand this complex problem. All the various possibilities which may interact to produce the observed behaviour must be considered: for example, has anything out of the ordinary happened during the day (or night) which may have caused anxiety or annoyance? Are the toilet facilities accessible and easy to locate? Is the elderly person on medication? Has there been a recent change in medication? Has there been a recent change in eating habits? Is the person drinking more fluids than usual? Does the resident appear unwell or in pain? Does the person suffer from poor eyesight or restricted mobility? Has there been a recent bereavement? Has the elderly person recently moved to new surroundings? How long has the incontinence been occurring? Did it start suddenly or gradually?

Life History

Secondly, you must also take into account the elderly confused person's life history, otherwise the toileting difficulties may be influenced by factors of which you are unaware.

In order to obtain a complete personal history (eg. previous lifestyle, habits at home and work, attitudes and expectations, sources of stress, methods of coping with change and stress, illnesses, pre-morbid toileting habits, normal pattern and frequency of micturition, etc), it is not only care staff who need to be involved in the process, but also the family of the confused person. Overall, the message for professional carers is 'know your clients'.

Recording the Information

The collection of all this information on possible contributory factors can be displayed on a record chart similar to the one shown below (with a covering sheet to provide space for a personal history):

DATE & TIME	A	B	C	BACKGROUND

The Procedure

This first stage in the management of incontinence and inappropriate urinating will help identify whether a consistent pattern exists. In order to get a clear picture, the behaviour should be monitored for a period of weeks in order to avoid making decisions on the basis of short-term fluctuations in behaviour. The information obtained should be shared with all carers, discussed during staff meetings and mentioned at 'handover' reports.

Taking time to assess the situation will help avoid the unjust labelling of an elderly confused person as incontinent following an isolated incident. Although behavioural difficulties do not appear as fully fledged problems but rather evolve from minor lapses, it does not follow that the odd slip in the complex toileting process inevitably signals the onset of incontinence. It is also wise to remember that the elderly confused are unlikely to provide a sensible explanation for their behaviour. So always be patient and open-minded when investigating the problem. Impatience may lead to false conclusions.

Misinterpreting the Problem

In a few cases inappropriate urinating may be the result of localised brain damage. Whilst brain dysfunction may result in memory loss and general intellectual deterioration, there are other impairments of neuropsychological function which would also interfere with the goal of continent behaviour. For example, a condition known as spatial agnosia, ie. an inability to recognise even familiar surroundings, can result in sufferers being unable to find their way to the toilet. Whilst it is possible to identify objects (eg. the urinal), localisation of them is damaged. Agnosic residents may be difficult to distinguish from the elderly confused who are disoriented as a result of memory impairment. Aphasic difficulties (ie. an impairment of communication), may prevent a patient asking to be taken to the toilet, or enquiring about directions, or being able to read signs which consist of words only. Difficulties with undressing may be the result of dressing apraxia, ie. a movement disorder which gives rise to an inability to relate clothes to person or to dissociate the clothes from the object on which they are placed, or to a failure to get the order right in dressing. The existence of a communicating hydrocephalus, which will always require medical investigation, is identified by the existence of intellectual deterioration, ataxia (unsteadiness whilst standing or walking) and incontinence.

Lack of consideration for the existence of such biological changes in the brain is bound to seriously interfere with efforts to manage the problem of incontinence. Therefore, assessment of the elderly person by a neuropsychologist should ideally be included in a thorough behavioural analysis, in order to establish the extent of memory loss and whether the presence of other neuropsychological deficits is contributing to the problem. This would avoid the risk of misinterpreting the nature of the behaviour, an error of judgement which would be easy to commit if it was automatically assumed that the elderly confused person possessed the neuro-psychological capabilities necessary to perform all the steps required to achieve continence. However as the expertise required to undertake a complete neuropsychological assessment is not readily available, an alternative option is to be aware of the potential existence of focal deficits, ie. those concentrated in one place. If close observation of the elderly person's behaviour suggests that it is not related to general intellectual impairment but may involve other forms of brain damage, then request the involvement of a specialist.

Clearly, whilst seeking an explanation can be a lengthy process, taking the trouble to understand a person's behaviour can save valuable time later. To intervene too quickly with inadequate information about the person and their problem, may not only be unhelpful, but is likely to result in the problem assuming crisis proportions.

Multiple Pathway

Despite a comprehensive problem analysis, identification of the cause of incontinence may remain difficult, especially when a mixture of reasons apply. It is likely that the majority of confused elderly people will suffer from many deficits and thus the first task must be to disentangle the multiple pathway. Furthermore, unlike other disruptive behaviours which are almost immediately obvious, behavioural analysis of incontinence and inappropriate urinating may be complicated by the hidden nature of the problem. It can be difficult to accurately identify an incident of incontinence at the time of its occurrence if, for example, the person is either discrete, indifferent or unaware of their bodily functions.

There are no simple solutions to these difficulties. Supporters will need to be especially observant during the observation period. It can be advisable to test various hypotheses *in succession* until the most appropriate explanation for the problem is found.

While the initial response may be to feel overwhelmed by the task of unravelling this complex handicap, successful identification of the factors involved can lead to behavioural improvement of benefit to both the sufferer and carers.

Therapy is the Art of the Possible

Following the period of observation, an accurate interpretation is essential because the information gathered during the behavioural analysis decides which method of solving the problem is most appropriate to the person and their situation. However, when interpreting the results of a behavioural analysis and deciding upon a plan of action carers must always take into account whether the circumstances responsible for the problem behaviour are not in turn the result of institutional restrictions, for example, managerial policy, staffing levels, staff attitudes, building design, etc. Without changes in the latter, attempts to change the former are likely to fail. It is a waste of time introducing a system of care if it will inevitably flounder on the bedrock of institutional rigidity.

Remember, the home exists for the benefit of residents. As far as is realistic, routines and policy should be flexible and centred upon the individual's needs. The objective must be to create an environment which maximises a resident's potential for independent functioning. In many cases this will involve the introduction of prosthetic aids to compensate for intellectual and physical deficits which cannot be resolved.

Keyword Summary

Seeking a detailed explanation
- A behaviour *unique* to an *individual.*
- Toileting involves a complex chain of skills
- ABC analysis of behaviour
  A = Activating event or situation
  B = Behaviour
  C = Consequence
- A detailed description of actual behaviour
- Background information
- Life history – involve the family
- Recording the information
- Finding a pattern – the procedure
- Avoid false accusations – be open-minded
- The risk of misinterpretation – the possible existence of focal brain damage
- Neuropsychological assessment

Multiple pathway
- Many deficits may be involved
- Monitoring can be difficult
- Be observant
- Test hypotheses *in succession*

Goal setting
- Realistic goals
- Small gains can be of considerable importance

Therapy is the art of the possible
- Accurate interpretation
- The obstacle of institutional restrictions
- Home exists for the benefit of residents
- Policy should be flexible
- Maximise independence
- Provide prostheses if necessary to compensate for disabilities

Management

Changing the Environment

Since an elderly person's surroundings can be responsible for the onset of inappropriate urinating, there is a need to adapt the environment in order to design-out the risk of this problem arising.

Building Familiarisation

To make it as easy as possible for residents to locate and use the toilet themselves, and thereby avoid the perplexing and distressing sensation of disorientation, the use of signs, symbols and 'pathfinder' arrows can be very effective in making a building more familiar. By creating a prosthetic environment a confused person who urinates inappropriately can be helped to achieve toilet use despite suffering from memory impairment.

Signs need to be placed in prominent positions and should be large enough to compensate for poor eyesight. Use simple messages—large pictorial signs or symbols are often better than just the written word. Personalise bedroom doors with the resident's name. Providing directional arrows or a coloured track along the wall between, for example, the day area and the toilet is important. There is little point labelling the entrance to the toilet if the only time residents are able to identify it is when they are standing in front of the door. They will also require 'the path' to the toilet to be signposted.

In addition to these special features, colour coding may also be helpful. By associating colours with different rooms, residents have an alternative key to the geography of the home.

You can imaginatively combine both colour coding and the use of symbols, to produce for example, the following results:

Room	Door	Directional Arrow	Symbol
Toilet	Blue	Blue	Blue 'T' on white background
Bathroom	White	White	White 'bath' on a blue background
Dining Room	Yellow	Yellow	Yellow 'knife and fork' on a black background
Day Room	Green	Green	Green 'scissors' on a yellow background
Bedroom	Orange	Orange	Orange 'bed' on a black background

There are numerous colour combinations, so you can make your choice blend in with the existing decorations and colour scheme. Always remember to use clear lettering and bright colours.

However, it is not enough to simply put up signs and symbols and expect the elderly residents to grasp the meaning. They must be taught to find their way about. You can introduce the information to a small number of residents in a Reality Orientation group. After this presentation in the 'classroom', staff should accompany confused residents around the home a few times. Eventually residents should be asked what comes next on the route. Also encourage residents to use their own cues. Get them to notice smells and noises which they can associate with the signs and symbols. This will help them build up a lasting mental map of the home.

Do not walk residents briskly from one location to another. They should learn at their own pace. The most confused will have the greatest difficulty remembering new information so teaching must take place regularly in order to increase the chances of learning taking place.

Be patient, speak slowly and use short simple sentences. If residents make mistakes, do not get irritated or critical. If they are successful, show pleasure and approval, but do not be patronising. When this period of orientation is over, give regular reminders about the geography of the home in everyday conversation. Although constant repetition may seem boring to you, it is not to the forgetful and confused.

The criticism that the introduction of orientation aids creates an institutional atmosphere is untrue. It is largely the attitudes of staff that are responsible for such an unhealthy development. To argue that such design changes would not be in accord with an aged person's own home ignores the fact that in nearly all cases the elderly confused in residential settings were unable to function in that living arrangement and this was the reason for their admission. Therefore, if nothing is done to compensate for the handicaps of this client population, in the misguided albeit well-intentioned belief that the 'homely' environment must not be defaced, disoriented residents may be subjected to a degrading and dependent existence.

At Night

Darkness can result in the problem of disorientation becoming acute. Waking up to 'blackness' can be alarming. What is familiar during the day can appear mysterious at night. Pioneering work over 40 years ago demonstrated that the increase in confusion at night was not the result of fatigue, but was the outcome of sensory deprivation, by showing that such confused behaviour could occur in a darkened room during daytime.

A solution is to install night lights in the bedroom and in areas the elderly person may wish to reach during the night, such as the toilet, so that the environment is gently illuminated. The use of a night light not only helps to reduce disorientation, but it also means that accidents are less likely to happen.

However, if finding the toilet is especially troublesome at night, as a last resort a commode can be provided by the bedside. Ensure that any embarrassment attached to the use of the commode is minimised. Of course, if residents' bedrooms were provided with en suite toilet and washing facilities, the likelihood of inappropriate urinating would be reduced and the indignity of using a commode would be avoided.

Removing Obstacles to Toilet Use

The layout of a residential or hospital setting should serve to reduce the number of barriers which make toilet use difficult or frustrating.

There must be an adequate number of toilets, bearing in mind that there will be several peak periods of usage during each day. Toilet facilities should be readily accessible at all times. They should be nearby (within approximately 10 to 15 yards), and the approach obstacle free, well lit and safe (eg. non-slip, free from spillage, with support rails, etc.). In residential homes the living arrangement most likely to minimise the problem of inaccessible toilets is to be found in group living units. The living area for a small group unit (optimum size 8 to 12 members) is relatively compact, so facilities are within easy reach. This could be a partial explanation for the anecdotal evidence that there is less incontinence in homes with group living arrangements when compared with traditional homes for the elderly.

All doors, whether they be, for example, the exit from a day room, or the entrance to the toilet, should be easy to open and wide enough to allow entry using a walking frame. Heavy doors will present a formidable barrier to progress. Nor should they be spring loaded as there is a risk that they will automatically rebound upon slow-moving residents passing through. Unfortunately inappropriate urinating may occur because toilets have been situated on the far side of heavy fire doors which are not easy for elderly confused people to open.

Equipment in the toilet area should be clean and well maintained. The toilet seat should be high enough for residents to get on and off easily. Hand rails either side of the toilet for extra support would also help. The toilet area should be private, warm and with plenty of room for manoeuvering walking aids; it should also be bright and adequately ventilated. Consideration should also be given to the design of the flushing system and washing facilities. The presence of a call system by the toilet would create a sense of confidence.

Away from the toilet area the provision of low-positioned, wide-seated chairs in a clutter-free lounge which allows for easy and safe movement around furniture would serve to further reduce the potential for environment-induced toileting difficulties. At night, bed-wetting which is the result of mobility problems or apathy can be alleviated by the introduction of beds which are fairly low (approximately 2 feet from the floor to the bed mattress), with firm mattresses and supports to aid standing. This would enable the elderly confused to get up during the night with comparative ease in order to take advantage of toilet facilities.

As you can see, changing the physical environment can help prevent inappropriate urinating occurring. Clearly it is a valuable option for working with the elderly confused who have toileting difficulties.

Keyword Summary

Designing-out inappropriate urinating

Building familiarisation
- Reduce disorientation
- The use of signs and directional cues
- Colour coding
- Learning the geography of a home
- Effective teaching techniques
- Regular reminders
- Orientation aids do not create institutionalisation
- A prosthetic or 'homely' environment?

At night
- An increase in disorientation
- The benefit of nightlights

Environmental obstacles
- Toilets – an adequate number and easily accessible
- A benefit of group living units – compact living space
- Doors should not be barriers
- Toilet areas – prosthetic, hospitable environment
- The lounge – allowing easy and safe movement
- Beds which facilitate toilet use

6

Reality Orientation

Whilst the introduction of memory aids and directional 'signposts' will increase a confused person's ability to find their way from one location to another, the process of orientation is further encouraged by ensuring that every staff-resident (or patient) interaction offers a tie with reality. Reality Orientation (RO) requires staff to consistently present current information on time, place and the identities of those around them, as well as a commentary on what is happening. Confused, rambling speech is either corrected or ignored. Although this approach to interaction is to be generally recommended, it is those residents who are mildly confused who will derive the greatest benefit.

Time, Place and Person Orientation

In conversation with an aged person who is confused and disoriented, always be in possession of accurate information. To be effective, information should be communicated to the individual naturally while daily activities are going on. Remind the person of the time, where they are and who you are. Explain all that is strange and do not take anything for granted. For example:

Time Orientation
'Mrs Wilson, it is 2 o'clock in the afternoon, do you wish to use the toilet?'

Place Orientation
'You have just walked out of the lounge, Mr Price. If you continue to follow the blue arrows along this corridor you will reach the toilet door which is also coloured blue.'

Person Orientation
'Mrs Kelly, my name is Beth. I work on this ward. Do you want me to call you Alice or Mrs Kelly?'

Since personal identity is such an important part of somebody's reality, always correctly identify the person. Whatever form of address is chosen, it should always be done consistently and respectfully. Initially, addressing the confused person by their title (Mr, Mrs or Miss) may help to promote self image.

To reduce anxiety, be friendly, patient and understanding. If appropriate, reassure them that their worries are groundless.

At night quietly talk to those who cannot sleep and reassure them about their whereabouts. Remind them that it is still night-time. However, you are likely to be at your lowest ebb if you have been awakened. Despite feeling tired and irritable, remember to be tolerant and speak softly and gently.

The most effective way to correct inaccurate and rambling speech is to help the elderly confused realise that their beliefs are mistaken and inappropriate. Be logical, polite and matter-of-fact in your approach. Help them discover the existence of errors by asking them to test reality. Do their statements coincide with the evidence? Tactfully disagree with misinterpretations of environmental input. Try to 'match' the level of conversation to the patient's ability to comprehend. Encourage them to examine their initial responses. If necessary, provide clues or partial information in order to jog their memory.

Your manner must always be non-threatening and supportive. If a correct response is given, reward with a smile or a simple gesture of approval. However, this is reality orientation *not* reality *con*frontation, so do not argue. If a disoriented resident cannot be persuaded, it is unwise to persist with your efforts. When practising RO you must always be aware of the consequences of challenging a confused person. Whilst it is easier to dispute impersonal information (eg. 'the toilet door is coloured blue, this door is yellow and leads to the dining room, not the toilet'), correcting emotionally significant statements (eg. 'you no longer live with your husband, Mrs Gregory. You live at an old people's home called Primrose House'), demands sensitivity and a knowledge of how the person would react to such a challenge.

The confused with sensory handicaps have a greater need for RO. If the problem of damaged hearing and poor eyesight cannot be corrected, compensate for these sensory losses by helping the confused identify reality through the use of all five senses: taste, smell, touch, hearing and vision.

This approach to RO, known as 24-hour, can be supplemented by a formal RO procedure within which current information is conveyed to, and discussed with, a small group using a board as a focus for details of date, place, weather, etc. Specific topics can be introduced, such as the meaning of building orientation aids, in order to help group members retain essential information despite their memory difficulties.

If RO is successful, a greater awareness of reality will reduce the risk of unacceptable toileting behaviour. This in turn can bring about a positive change in confidence and self respect, thereby consolidating the return to continence.

Keyword Summary

Reality orientation (RO)
- Offering a tie with reality
- Mildly confused benefit the most
- Time, place and person orientation
- Be friendly, patient and understanding
- Be logical and matter-of-fact
- Reality testing
- Tactfully disagree with misinterpretations
- If necessary provide clues
- It is *not* reality *con*frontation
- RO demands sensitivity
- Helping those with sensory handicaps
- Formal (classroom) RO
- A positive change in confidence and self respect

7

Behavioural Methods

Behavioural management has shown itself to be a powerful means of modifying problem behaviour. This approach to care systematically manipulates the social consequences (C) of the unwanted behaviour in order to reduce the frequency of occurrence. It can be especially useful in managing attention-seeking and apathetic behaviours.

Unfortunately, behavioural programmes designed to control inappropriate urinating have been only partially successful with the confused elderly. However, as behavioural management brings into existence a highly desirable structure and consistency of approach which allows for a positive development in the relationship between carer and client, it should not be dismissed out of hand. In practice, staff attend to and expect desirable and appropriate behaviour, rather than give attention to unwanted behaviours. If a decision is made to introduce a behavioural system of management, only those elderly confused who have the capacity to be continent, but are not motivated to do so, should be involved.

Behaviour Modification

A reward system

In general, the basic idea is to deny the elderly confused person fuss and attention after discovering evidence of incontinence or inappropriate urinating. Even angry and critical responses from staff may be counter-productive. They may actually be rewarding and thereby encourage further episodes of incontinent behaviour. However, the wetness cannot be completely ignored. Some action is inevitable. Keep your feelings under control. Whilst the person's clothing is being changed, try to deal with the situation in a matter-of-fact manner. Prompt the person to get changed as far as is possible independently so they take a degree of responsibility for correcting the consequences of their incontinence.

However, ignoring incontinent behaviour can only be a partial strategy. What is also needed is a system of rewarding appropriate behaviour.

i) **Praise and prompt.** To encourage continent behaviour, a programme of reinforcement (ie. a reward) for being dry, and prompted toileting can be introduced.

The procedure involves establishing check times throughout the day, for example, at two hour intervals, to see whether the resident is wet or dry. If the person is dry, reward them with your approval and a few minutes of conversation. Explain why you are pleased. In this way you are not simply ignoring the problem and hoping behavioural change will occur, but you are also providing an opportunity for the person to learn more appropriate behaviour.

Following the check, which should be carried out in a discrete manner in order to avoid humiliation, remind them to visit the toilet. If the goal of the programme is to encourage continent behaviour, but not independent toileting, accompany or assist them to the toilet. If the patient uses the toilet, then once again show approval. In this way you are encouraging appropriate toilet use. However, if the person is being taken to the toilet after being discovered wet at the check time, continue with the same matter-of-fact approach adopted whilst their clothing was being changed. Using the toilet after being incontinent cannot really be considered a target behaviour worthy of reward.

When giving praise continue to be aware that you should not treat the elderly person as a child or appear condescending. This may not only serve to annoy but may easily undermine confidence. When communicating with an elderly person, the aim must always be to maintain their self respect and dignity.

However, this method of control will only work if what is given as a reward is seen by confused residents as rewarding and pleasurable. It is not *your* opinion which is paramount. Whilst the approval and attention of a carer may sometimes be a reward in itself, this is not always enough. In this situation you will have to enrich the life of the incontinent resident by providing small tangible rewards which can either be used or consumed (although always combine such reinforcers with a social reward such as praise). Whatever type of reward is chosen, it must be in addition to what is theirs by right, and should not include privileges which are routinely accessible to all.

Always consider the relevance of the rewards. If a resident is being rewarded with food it would not be very effective if the person has just eaten a meal. Similarly, choosing a reward which is readily available anyway is unlikely to be a potent reinforcer of desired behaviour. It therefore makes sense to have a collection of rewards which can be drawn upon to match the demands of the situation. An alternative option is to involve a resident in a token economy. This involves tokens being given to a resident after they have been found dry, which can be exchanged at a later time for back-up rewards of differing token value. This method enables a person to take advantage of their reinforcement preferences which may change over time. The financial cost of token economy programmes (TEPs) is small and thus they have a practical relevance for NHS hospitals and Social Services' residential homes for the elderly.

Any reward should be given immediately. If there is a delay, the person may not remember why they are being rewarded and so inappropriate urinating will continue. It is a strength of TEPs that the tokens are easily dispensed and can be given immediately after the desired behaviour. This can be a problem with some other material rewards.

When 'dry' behaviour and appropriate toilet use have become well established, you can gradually withdraw the tangible rewards and rely solely on 'natural' social reinforcers. It is for this reason that material reinforcers should be used in tandem with praise and approval, for these social actions will eventually be of paramount significance. People are rewarding and failing to reward each other all the time, often without realising it. What behavioural management does is to use everyday social phenomena in a structured manner to bring about and maintain continent behaviour. In this way the target behaviour is 'trapped' by 'natural' social consequences and the artificial system of material rewards may be withdrawn.

ii) **Independent toileting.** Following a check the goal may also be to encourage independent toileting. This can be achieved in a number of ways:

Increasing opportunity
You can increase the probability that residents will use the toilet independently by sitting them near the facilities rather than far away from them. To familiarise residents with the location, take them for a walk in the vicinity of the toilet area. If they are seated with residents who toilet appropriately, these people will be effective models for the desired behaviour. The positive reactions of staff to these able residents will be a further incentive to adopt similar behaviours.

Shaping
This technique involves rewarding actions which gradually approximate the target behaviour, ie. independent toileting. Intermediate goals are set in order to eventually achieve the main goal. If the steps between each goal are small, there will be an easy transition between one target and the next. In this way the person obtains

the toilet resulted in the voiding of urine or not. It is desirable to keep the number of occasions when voiding does not occur to a minimum and thus there is a need to identify those visits to the toilet which were unnecessary.

If a pattern of micturition is revealed over a number of days (at least three), then the confused resident is a suitable candidate for habit retraining. At those times when the resident was found to be consistently wet, adjustments are made to the schedule to allow them to void before incontinence occurs. Similarly visits to the toilet may be discontinued if a resident has regularly failed to void when taken to the toilet. In this way the programme is amended according to the individual's needs.

For example, the following results may be obtained:

	8.00 am	10.00 am	12.00 am	2.00 pm	4.00 pm	6.00 pm	8.00 pm
Check	Wet	Wet	Dry	Dry	Wet	Wet	Dry
Toilet Use	Yes	No	Yes	No	No	Yes	No

Observation has revealed episodes of incontinence at 8.00 am., 10.00 am., 4.00 pm. and 6.00 pm., and non-usage of the toilet at 10.00 am., 2.00 pm., 4.00 pm. and 8.00 pm.

To pre-empt incontinent behaviour, the schedule is adjusted so that toilet prompts take place one hour earlier than the original check times when the person was discovered wet. In addition, those checks when the patient was found to be dry but the prompt to use the toilet did *not* result in the voiding of urine, are now discontinued.

The resulting schedule of toilet prompts is as follows: 7.00 am., 9.00 am., 12.00 noon, 3.00 pm. and 5.00 pm.

As you can see, the number of voiding times has been reduced to five from the original seven. So not only does this procedure benefit residents, but it also allows for a more efficient use of staff time. It is important to bear in mind that once retraining starts it should not be interrupted.

The final stage in habit retraining is to extend the intervals between prompts by 15 minutes until three-hourly intervals are established throughout the 12 hour day. Following a successful outcome to this stage, prompted toileting has been reduced to just four times daily.

As a result of adjusting and extending the time between toileting - prompts so that voiding is postponed for as long as possible, a new pattern of predictable micturition is established which enables the confused person to remain dry, as well as avoid fruitless journeys to the toilet. The advantages for both dependent and carer are easy to appreciate.

The Enuresis Alarm

To resolve the problem of bed-wetting at night, the more able elderly confused might benefit from the alarm device known as the 'bell and pad' procedure which is generally successful in treating enuretic children.

This method, which was first described nearly 50 years ago, provides the opportunity for the aged dependent to learn once again to discriminate while asleep a level of bladder volume and pressure that is below the level of automatic discharge which results in incontinence.

As soon as a urine-sensitive pad fitted below the bed sheet is moistened by urine a bell wakes the person up. The noise serves to inhibit further urination in the bed by causing the bladder muscles to automatically contract. The person must then go to the toilet (if they need to be accompanied, a bedside 'call' system will be required to alert staff). An alternative would be to use a urinal in those instances where poor mobility makes getting out of bed difficult. After voiding the person returns to sleep.

With repeated presentations, the person associates a level of bladder fullness with the bell ringing and waking up. Eventually they learn to respond to internal cues and wake up just before the alarm is triggered. After fourteen consecutive dry nights the alarm can be removed. Each dry night should be reinforced with praise.

While the alarm must be sufficiently loud to wake the person, it must not be unnecessarily distressing or intrusive. Instead of a bell, a buzzer or pillow-shaker may be used. Tactile alarms are especially useful for the person who would be embarrassed by a private mishap being transferred into a public event.

Both staff and the confused resident must be able to understand how the equipment operates and the aims of the programme. For example, the resident or night-staff will have to turn the alarm off, the instrument will have to be reset, and the pad will have to be wiped off and a dry sheet placed on the pad. The person must be able to wake up sufficiently to toilet appropriately and therefore if the person is a heavy sleeper there will need to be careful supervision by night-staff. The use of night medication, which might be responsible for the problem, can seriously interfere with the procedure.

While this method is not of proven use with the confused elderly, it is worth considering in those cases where nocturnal enuresis is associated with a mild degree of intellectual impairment. The use of portable enuresis alarms has been advocated for day-time practice as a means of reliably observing bladder function, as well as allowing re-learning to occur. However, the use of an alarm would be humiliating and degrading, whilst the introduction of an alternative device which does not cause embarrassment (ie. a small transmitter worn under clothing that emits a signal when urine is passed) has yet to be evaluated. Overall, the method remains best suited to the problem of secondary nocturnal enuresis.

Keyword Summary

Habit retraining
- Pattern of micturition guides the toileting programme
- Inflexible toileting procedures are not always to be recommended
- Objective is to anticipate incontinence
- A socially acceptable toileting rhythm
- Check and prompt
- Habit Retraining Assessment Chart
- Who is a suitable candidate?
- Adjusting the schedule
- An individualised programme
- Reducing the number of toilet prompts
- Advantages for both residents and staff

The enuresis alarm
- 'Bell & Pad' procedure
- Learning to respond to internal muscular cues
- The need for various types of alarm
- All involved need to understand the procedure
- Method is not proven with the confused elderly
- Portable enuresis alarms – impractical at present

The Multi-Modal Approach

In a residential or hospital setting the multiple pathway to incontinence and inappropriate urinating can often be best confronted through the provision of a range of management techniques which are offered as part of routine care policy. This is known as the multi-modal approach. It provides a comprehensive management regime which trawls the potential causes of incontinent behaviour and offers both ward-or-unit-based procedures and individualised intervention programmes.

In addition to the prosthetic and therapeutic initiatives discussed in earlier chapters, the following suggestions are further examples of 'good' management practice.

On admission

Admission to a residential setting can involve worry, stress and even crisis. The breakdown of relationships, loss of possessions and disruption of routines can all be threatening experiences. Residential homes are rarely havens of stability and tranquillity, characterised as they are by staff changes and a loss of privacy. The outcome can be anxiety-based difficulties and depression.

To minimise the potential for trauma there should be sympathetic preparation and a careful, and possibly phased, admission. In this way adjustment anxieties are contained. The elderly confused should be welcomed with sensitivity. All care staff who will be involved with the new resident should be aware of their needs and idiosyncracies. Such good admission procedures can prevent the onset of emotionally related incontinent behaviour which is sometimes observed within a short period after admission.

Medical examination

Ensure that the incontinent resident is examined by a GP and that all medical problems are treated.

Drugs

All drugs being taken at the time of admission should be reviewed. If the person is on diuretics are they being administered at the optimum times? If tranquillizers or sleeping tablets are prescribed they need to be the minimal quantity of the mildest agent effective to either provide calmness or ensure sleep but which also allow normal micturition to occur.

Mobility and sensory handicaps

If a resident's mobility needs to be improved, is the involvement of a physiotherapist or chiropodist required? Would walking aids be of use? Is there a need to correct, or compensate for visual deficits?

Diet

To avoid constipation, does the residents' diet provide enough roughage? Regular consumption of fruit, vegetables, and bread and breakfast cereals which contain fibre are recommended. Do you need the assistance of a dietician?

Fluids

Drinking habits should always be observed as there is a need for an adequate daily fluid intake. Some residents drink too much, while others may drink too little. If necessary maintain an accurate record of intake and output.

Night-time routines

There is certainly a need for staff to ensure that residents urinate before going to bed. Is there also a need to restrict drinks two to three hours before a resident who suffers from nocturnal enuresis retires? During the night check regularly whether residents are awake and wishing to use the toilet. The decision to wake residents who regularly wet the bed so they can pass urine appropriately must be considered alongside the possible resulting problems of disorientation, resistance and daytime fatigue.

The Provision of Care

Many requests to be toileted are false alarms often occurring at busy times on a ward or unit. As these are likely to represent manipulative demands for attention, reward appropriate non-demanding behaviour with your time. A constructive approach would be to involve residents in a programme of stimulation and activity which reflects individual needs and brings enjoyment and the opportunity for achievement. The outcome will be a decrease in time-consuming demands and an increase in mutually rewarding staff-resident contact. Group living arrangements appear to encourage such developments.

On occasions the problem is not excessive demands but a reluctance to ask. When staff do not wear uniform, be aware that a resident may be too embarrassed to request assistance in case they mistakenly seek help from a visitor.

If the elderly confused are not allowed to exercise their toileting skills because cleanliness and hygiene take on a disproportionate importance for care staff, there will be an unnecessary increase in dependency as residents lose the motivation to care for themselves. Give them as much responsibility for their own care as is realistic. Adequate staffing is obviously required as elderly confused residents should not be hurried as they attempt to maintain independence and this can involve scarce staff resources monitoring an individual for a lengthy period of time. Always reward behaviour whenever the toilet is spontaneously used.

The severely confused who have lost bladder control and who unfortunately do not reveal a pattern of micturition must still be kept dry. As habit retraining cannot be practised, a rigid toileting regime will need to be implemented at regular intervals throughout the day.

Dressing

A person's dressing ability should be assessed and, if necessary, practice in dressing skills should be provided. It may be advantageous to arrange for clothing adaptations. Velcro fastenings to replace buttons can assist the confused elderly who have toileting difficulties because of dressing problems. For women, a loose skirt and loose elastic in the waistband of underwear are easy and quick to manage. For men, trousers with a long fly and easy fastening are recommended. However, always remember that normal clothing should be worn, for personal appearance plays a large part in determining how others react and this in turn influences self-respect.

Incontinence Aids

If patients use commodes during the day they must be screened from public view and complete privacy guaranteed. The commode should have a wide base for stability, a firm padded back and arm rests and for the person's ease of transfer should be the same height as the chair or bed. The advice of an occupational therapist can be very helpful in such matters.

When incontinence is not amenable to therapeutic intervention (apart from rigid toileting) personal protection may be advisable. The type of protection will depend upon the amount and occasions of bladder discharge, ie. whether they occur during the day or night, and whether they occur whilst the patient is up and dressed, or in bed.

Other factors which will need to be considered include the severity of confusion and the degree of mobility and dexterity.

The multi-modal approach to management has shown itself to be very successful providing as it does a global response to this complex and difficult problem leaving no stone unturned.

Keyword Summary

The multi-modal approach
- A comprehensive management regime
- Good admissions procedure
- Medical examination
- Drugs
- Mobility and sensory handicaps
- Diet
- Fluids
- Night-time routines
- The provision of care:
  - stimulation and activity programmes
  - maintain independence
  - rigid toileting procedure
- Dressing
- Incontinence aids

SECTION 3
The Supporters

Helpful Attitudes

Be Positive

Positive staff attitudes are the key to the success of most of the ideas discussed in this book. It does not matter how effective these methods appear in theory, if the attitudes of those who are putting them into practice are unhelpful, they are destined to fail. Disinterest in the client group or a belief that efforts to improve the situation are pointless are clearly counterproductive.

Be tolerant, patient and tactful. Continue to respect the individual. Do not over-react or feel overwhelmed by having responsibility for a resident who is incontinent or urinates inappropriately.

Without being too optimistic, expect improvement. It can occur; deterioration is not inevitable. Time and time again, the behaviour of the elderly confused improves when thoughtful management is introduced.

Do not discourage residents from taking responsibility for themselves and exercising independence. Caring for their physical welfare is only part of the job. Paying attention to their emotional and social needs is also of great importance.

Try not to be rigid in your beliefs, and if necessary, readjust your attitudes and expectations. If new care techniques are recommended, do not automatically regard it as a criticism of what may have been accepted previously as good management.

The Whole Person

Incontinence is not simply a problem to be managed. It is a personal difficulty the elderly resident requires help to overcome. Consider the whole person. Whilst they may have an unwanted behaviour, include this in an appreciation of the person as an individual with a colourful history and a wealth of achievements. A person who has needs, feelings, likes and dislikes.

Even though confusion may be a barrier to communication and thus make it difficult to appreciate how experiences have shaped an elderly person's life, an interest in the whole individual helps you to better understand the aged resident. This must inevitably lead to an improvement in the quality of care you provide.

Burn-out

When many confused elderly people are gathered together problems can appear insurmountable. To manage one incontinent resident may be difficult, to care for several can appear impossible. Incontinence and inappropriate urinating can be 24-hour problems which demand much greater commitment from carers than other disruptive behaviours.

You may approach your work with enthusiasm, yet soon become dismayed and discouraged by the physical demands, unsocial hours and inadequate support. It is frequently forgotten that staff require praise and encouragement.

In these situations you need to share your anger, disappointment and grievances. If you do not, you risk experiencing 'burnout'—feelings of frustration, exhaustion, demoralisation and hopelessness. So, as a regular practice, seek the mutual support of colleagues. Hold group meetings to exchange experiences and concerns. Do not feel embarrassed to acknowledge your doubts and weaknesses, for you will also undoubtedly have assets and strengths your fellow carers may benefit from.

However, if you work in relative isolation and there is little chance of assistance from other carers, try and develop coping attitudes. Dismiss negative and self-defeating ideas. Do not let your mind run riot to an extent where you cannot 'see the wood for the trees'. Be constructive and concentrate on the task at hand. The demands and pressures may appear endless but you will only successfully get on top of them if you tackle one problem at a time. Positive thinking can help prevent undesirable levels of stress and strain.

Overall, adopting the right attitudes can make you a more effective carer, and as a result help the elderly confused obtain a better quality of life.

Keyword Summary

Attitudes
- Be positive
- Respect the residents
- Do not over-react
- Remain confident that improvement will occur
- Encourage independence
- Do not be threatened by 'new' ideas

The whole person
- Treat the resident as a person, not simply as a problem
- Take an interest in the whole person; appreciate needs and feelings

Burn-out
- Problems appear insurmountable
- Enthusiasm replaced by dismay
- Staff need praise and encouragement
- Burn-out – feelings of exhaustion and frustration
- The need for the support of colleagues
- Coping attitudes – dismiss negative ideas
- Be constructive – tackle one problem at a time

Being the 'Therapist'

Not Just a Carer

As we have seen the effective management of incontinent behaviour is not something that can be switched on and off. It needs to be practised day in, day out. Such a demand for a '24-hour therapy' inevitably involves nurses and residential workers.

The routine work of care staff in daily contact and communication with the elderly person means they have a major impact on management. Only those working so closely with the problem can identify the most likely explanations and possible solutions. The more familiar you and your colleagues are with the elderly resident, the more accurate your knowledge will be. Nobody else can possibly be so well informed. No other professional can appreciate the difficulties that arise from day to day. In practice you therefore cease to be simply a carer and become a skilled 'therapist' in your own right.

Strategy

Below are guidelines for all therapeutic supporters:

1. Identify the reason for the toileting difficulties.
2. Make a plan to resolve them. Whenever possible involve the resident. Success is often determined

by the motivation which exists to become continent, and this can be favourably influenced if there is co-operation between staff and resident.

3. Put the plan into action.
4. Evaluate the extent to which the plan is effective. Monitor the effect the intervention is also having on the aged person's overall performance and welfare.

Such an approach is not only likely to reduce the burden of responsibility but will also improve your own skills and increase the satisfaction you get from your job.

Keyword Summary

More than a carer
- Good management practice cannot be switched on and off
- 24-hour therapy
- Effective management requires accurate information
- Nurses and care-staff are the best informed
- Being a skilled 'therapist'

Therapeutic strategy
- Find the cause
- Design a treatment plan
- Put plan into operation
- Evaluate the outcome

Managing the Problem at Home

There are around 500,000 confused elderly people in Britain, yet less than a quarter of them are cared for in hospitals or residential homes. This means, without any doubt, that the family is the main provider of care. Typically, the responsibility lies with a partner, daughter or daughter-in-law. Yet relatives struggling to cope with behaviour often as difficult as that found in institutional settings are frequently the forgotten sufferers.

Although nobody outside the situation really knows what it is like to live with a person who has toileting difficulties, it is hoped that many of the ideas described in this book will make the task of caring easier. To end this practical guide, here are a few more points to help relatives cope with their unenviable situation.

Coping with Feelings

Although caring for a confused relative who is incontinent or urinates inappropriately is a common problem, generally the difficulties are well tolerated. However, sometimes the responsibility can become oppressive and feelings of unhappiness and upset come to the fore. It is easy to react with disgust at your loved one's unhygienic habits at such times, and then experience guilt at being disgusted. Do not be ashamed of these feelings. Although you might feel embarrassed, nothing will be gained by keeping the problem a secret from family and friends.

It is understandable to grieve for the loss of companionship as major personality changes occur in those you love. The confused relative who is incontinent can appear even less like the person who was once known and loved. Your relationship may no longer be mutually rewarding. To help overcome feelings of loneliness why not seek the company of a Relative Support Group?

Anger is a common and natural response when coping with incontinence. Your relative may appear uncharacteristically lazy. Despite blatant evidence to the contrary, they may deny or appear unaware of the incontinent episode. Implausible excuses and explanations may be offered. Whilst these may represent the thinking of an increasingly forgetful and confused individual, denial may also be a deliberate 'therapeutic' response. The elderly confused have feelings and thus can experience fear and shame. Behaving in a manner acceptable only in the first years of life can generate irrational and desperate attempts to preserve self-respect. So try to be angry with the behaviour and not the person.

You may also be angry with fate having been so unkind. You may be resentful with other members of the family who are not 'pulling their weight'. If you are unable to contain your discontent, you obviously need to do something. Share your feelings and demand support or relief.

Some carers can become so enmeshed in their situation that life can appear a never-ending round of supervision and responsibility. It can help if you try to emotionally distance yourself from your problem. When you feel stressed and anxious check whether your worries are largely unfounded or exaggerated. Ask yourself whether there is any evidence to support your fears. Abandon 'what if . . .' thoughts. Reduce the pressure you feel by avoiding such ideas as 'I shouldn't be doing this' or 'I must do that'. Such thoughts increase the demands you place on yourself and make caring even more tiring. Toileting difficulties can be bad enough to handle without your inflicting more and more pressure upon yourself.

Some carers benefit from placing not only an emotional distance between themselves and their caring responsibilities, but also, on occasions, a physical distance. Whenever possible get out, do things, meet people and generally have a break from what may at times be an upsetting and demanding routine.

Resources

Do not be reluctant to seek professional help. Contact your GP or local Social Services' office to request practical support. You could be helped by the services offered by a district nurse, social worker or community occupational therapist.

A visit from a district nurse can be arranged by your GP. They will deal with minor health complaints, as well as being able to supply incontinence pads and pants, some of which are disposable. The nurse can also provide and advise on the use of incontinence sheets to protect bedding. There might be a night nursing service to help lift, toilet and change your loved one. It is also possible that there is a nurse incontinence adviser in your area who will be able to discuss management and supply a range of protective aids.

You can contact via your local Social Services' office a community occupational therapist. These specialists provide mobility aids to remedy unsteadiness and help people who are prone to falls. They are also able to assess the home situation and spot potential hazards and obstacles. For example, does the arrangement of bedroom furniture allow the person to move around safely? They can arrange for the loan of a commode, and assist supporters in obtaining a range of prosthetic aids such as handrails, raised toilet seats, etc. Occupational therapists are also trained to teach people who suffer from limited mobility how to move more easily and less painfully, as well as teaching them, for example, how to stand up from a comfortable armchair in order to start their journey to appropriate toileting. They can also teach you how to lift without causing injury to yourself.

A social worker will be able to advise you whether the amount of care you provide during the day or night, or the burden of laundry costs, entitles you to additional state benefits and allowances. They will know whether there is an incontinence laundry service or a collection facility for disposable pads and sheeting. If major renovation work is required in order to allow your confused relative to live at home (eg. a toilet may be needed on the ground floor), a social worker will provide information on DHSS grants available.

The Citizens Advice Bureau may have useful tips about local facilities. If you want information about the nature of the problem you are dealing with, there are voluntary organisations such as the Alzheimer's Disease Society which are only too willing to provide guidance. It is often the case that receiving an explanation can give great relief.

If you are going to provide good care, you must always consider your own needs. Increasing the resources available to you can reduce the cost of caring and ensure that you are able to continue in your supporting role. Encourage other family members to help you share out the responsibility. Do any relatives live close at hand? Could they occasionally come over and keep a watchful eye while you have a day or evening out?

Finally, never feel guilty about no longer being able to be the sole care giver, or your inability to manage without help. These are irrational and self-destructive beliefs. Nobody expects you to be either superhuman or a martyr.

Practical Suggestions

Relatives often complain that they do not receive practical guidance on how best to cope with the problem of confusion. Yet this can so easily be provided in a straightforward way. For example, always remember that simple, predictable and familiar routines help reduce the likelihood of confused behaviour.

Work at trying to improve your loved one's memory. This can be aided by having a place for everything and putting everything in its place. Make sure there is easy access to everyday information. For example, put up a 'memory board' in the kitchen or any other prominent place. Make sure you include information on the day's activities and especially details of your movements and whereabouts. This is essential if you plan to go out for this will help reduce feelings of separation anxiety. Try to make your absence from home predictable. When left alone, always leave your relative with something to do to occupy their mind.

If your loved one wears a watch, make sure it is accurate. If they are fit and able, encourage them to do chores around the house. This will not only give them interest but will reduce their dependence upon you. If confidence can be gained from being involved in the domestic routine, your relative is less likely to feel vulnerable if you need to leave them alone.

Although incontinence and inappropriate urinating can make life particularly difficult for supporting relatives, always remain confident that improvement may occur. Use the information in this book to open your mind to ideas and practical suggestions which you may never have considered. It may enable you to make the best of what must often seem an impossible situation.

Keyword Summary

The forgotten sufferers
- The family is the main provider of care

Coping
- Do not be ashamed of your feelings
- Do not keep the problem a secret
- Grief is understandable
- Seek the company of a Relative Support Group
- Anger is a natural reaction – be angry at the behaviour, not the person
- Share your feelings
- Emotional distance can be helpful
- Are your worries justified?
- Abandon 'what if' thoughts
- Watch out for the pressure words – I *must*, I *should*, etc.
- Take a break

Resources
- Seek professional help: General practitioner; District nurse; Occupational therapist; Social worker
- Citizens Advice Bureau may have useful information
- Voluntary organisations
- Recruit family members to help out
- Needing help – do not feel guilty
- You are not superhuman
- Do not be a martyr

Practical suggestions
- Simple and predictable routines are helpful
- A place for everything, and everything in its place
- Memory board
- Make absences from home predictable
- Clocks and watches – are they accurate?
- Promote independence
- Going out – provide occupation
- Open your mind to ideas

———◇———

Appendix I

Useful Organisations

Alzheimer's Disease Society, 3rd Floor, Bank Buildings, Fulham Broadway, London SW6 1EP

Age Concern England, Bernard Sunley House, Pitcairn Road, Mitcham, Surrey CR4 3LL

Age Concern Scotland, 33 Castle Street, Edinburgh EH2 3DN

Age Concern Wales, 1 Park Grove, Cardiff CF1 3B

Association of Carers, Medway Homes, Balfour Road, Rochester, Kent ME4 6QU

Coventry Association for the Carers of the Elderly Confused, Newfield Lodge Day Centre, Kingfield Road, Coventry CV1 4DW

Disabled Living Foundation, 346 Kensington High Street, London W14 8NS

Help the Aged, 16-18 St James Walk, London EC1R 0BE

National Council for Carers and their Elderly Dependants, 29 Chilworth Mews, London W2 3RG

Appendix II

Further Reading for Carers

Forgetfulness in Elderly Persons—Advice for Carers, Age Concern.

Coping with Caring—A Guide to Identifying and Supporting an Elderly Person with Dementia, Brian Lodge, MIND, 1981.

24-Hour Approach to the Problem of Confusion in Elderly People, Una Holden et al, Winslow Press, Bicester, 1980.

Our Elders, G. K. Wilcock & J. A. Muir Gray, Oxford University Press, 1981.

Coping with Ageing Parents, C. J. Gilleard & G. Watt, MacDonald Ltd., Loanhead, Midlothian, 1983.

Thinking It Through, U. Holden, Winslow Press, Bicester, 1984.

Caring for the Person with Dementia, Alzheimer's Disease Society, 1984.

Living with Dementia, C. J. Gilleard, Croom Helm Ltd., Beckenham, Kent, 1984.

The 36-Hour Day, N. L. Mace & P. V. Rabins, Hodder & Stoughton, London, 1985.